Contents

How to use this book   2

A2   Counting in Is, I0s and I00s   3

A2   Odd and even   4

A2   Ordinal numbers   5

A2   Comparing numbers   6

B2   Adding pairs to I0, 9, 8, 7 and 6   7

B2   Adding 3 numbers   8

C2   Block graphs   9

C2   Pictographs   I0

D2   3D shapes   II–I2

D2   Counting back in I0s   I3

D2   Adding or subtracting 9   I4

E2   Odd and even   I5

E2   Twos and fives   I6

E2   Multiplying and dividing

E2   Dividing   I8

A3   Hundreds, tens and units   I9

A3   Rounding   20

A3   Adding   2I

A3   Difference   22

B3   Shape patterns   23

B3   Fractions   24

B3   Making I0 and I00   25

B3   Making the next I0   26

C3   Adding and subtracting   27

D3   Adding   28

D3   Subtracting   29

E3   Dividing   30

E3   Multiplying and dividing   3I

E3   Doubling and halving   32

How to use this book

Each page has a title telling you what it is about.

Instructions look like this. Always read these carefully before starting.

This shows you how to set out your work. The first question is done for you.

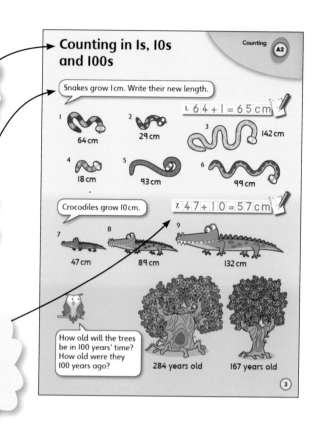

Read these word problems very carefully. Decide how you will work out the answers.

This is Owl. Ask your teacher if you need to do his questions.

Counting in 1s, 10s and 100s

Snakes grow 1 cm. Write their new length.

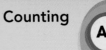

1. $64 + 1 = 65$ cm

1 64 cm

2 29 cm

3 142 cm

4 18 cm

5 93 cm

6 99 cm

Crocodiles grow 10 cm.

7. $47 + 10 = 57$ cm

7 47 cm

8 89 cm

9 132 cm

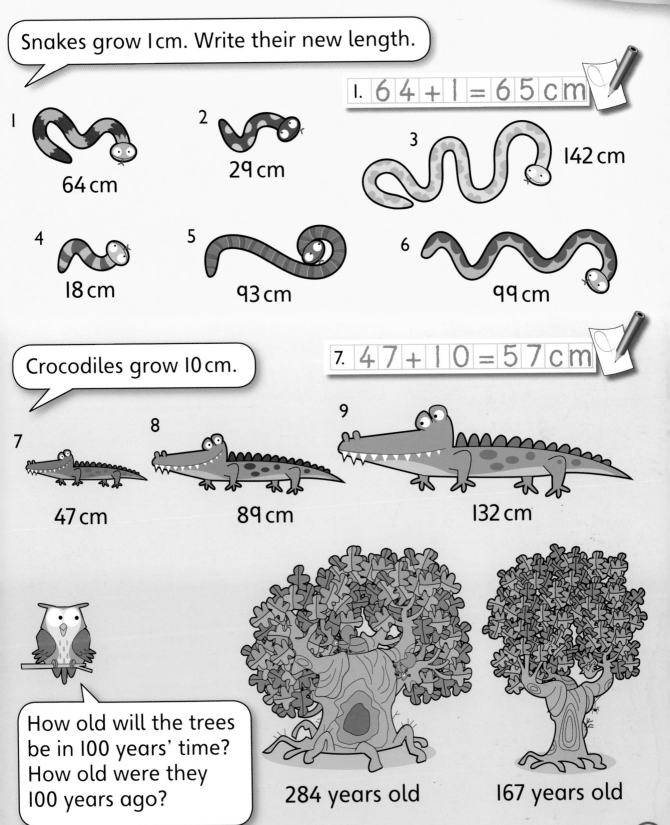

How old will the trees be in 100 years' time? How old were they 100 years ago?

284 years old

167 years old

Odd and even

Write the even numbered raffle tickets.

1. 46, 48, 50, 52

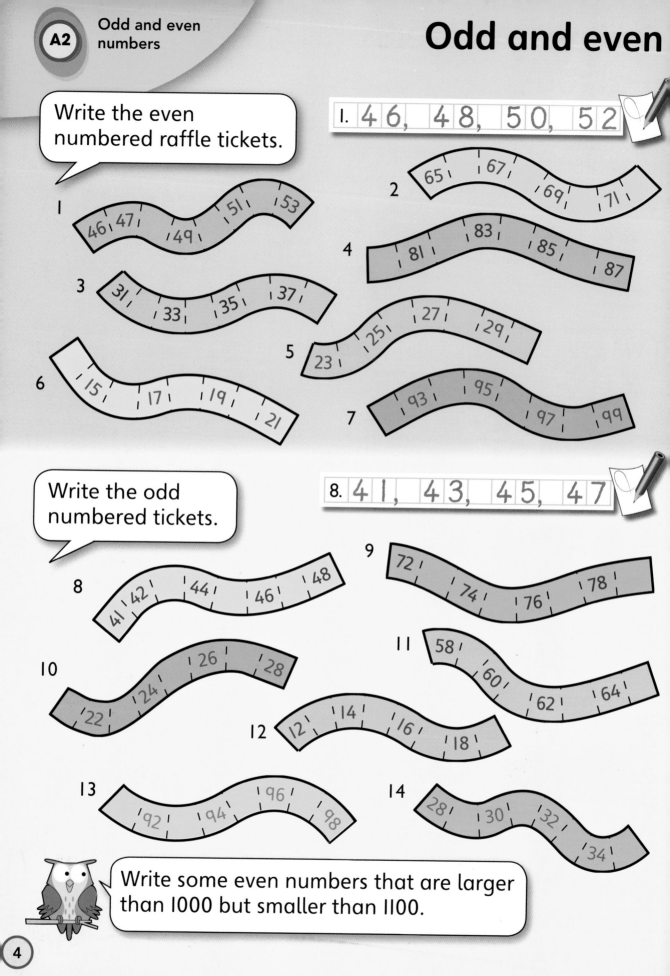

1 46 47 49 51 53

2 65 67 69 71

4 81 83 85 87

3 31 33 35 37

5 23 25 27 29

6 15 17 19 21

7 93 95 97 99

Write the odd numbered tickets.

8. 41, 43, 45, 47

8 41 42 44 46 48

9 72 74 76 78

10 22 24 26 28

11 58 60 62 64

12 12 14 16 18

13 92 94 96 98

14 28 30 32 34

Write some even numbers that are larger than 1000 but smaller than 1100.

Ordinal numbers

> Write the letter for these positions in the line.

1. d

1	First	2	Fourth	3	Tenth

4	Ninth	5	Sixth	6	Eleventh
7	Eighth	8	Thirteenth	9	Second

> Write the position of:

10. Third

10   11   12   13

> Write your whole name. What is the third letter?
> What positions are the other letters?
> Do any two positions have the same letter?

Comparing numbers

Write each set of numbers in order, from the smallest to the largest.

1. 18, 23, 31

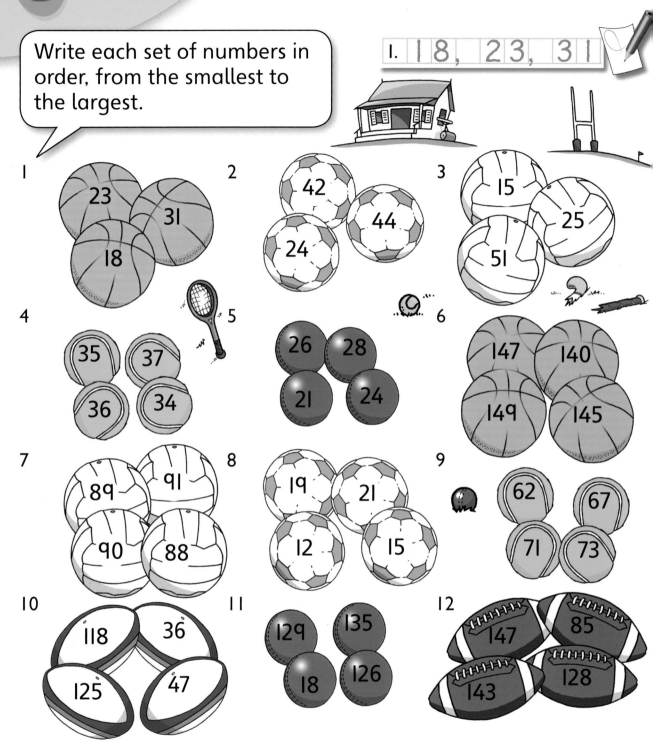

1.
23 31 18

2.
42 44 24

3.
15 25 51

4.
35 37 36 34

5.
26 28 21 24

6.
147 140 149 145

7.
89 91 90 88

8.
19 21 12 15

9.
62 67 71 73

10.
118 36 125 47

11.
129 135 18 126

12.
147 85 143 128

Write the largest number from each set. Then write them in order, from the smallest to the largest. Repeat for the smallest numbers in each set.

Adding pairs to 10, 9, 8, 7 and 6

How much more to make 10p in each purse?

1. $6p + 4p = 10p$

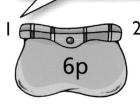

1

6p

2

8p

3

5p

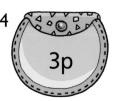

4

3p

5

1p

The flags show how many cars there are in each ghost train. How many cars are in the tunnel?

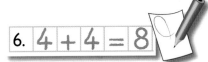

6. $4 + 4 = 8$

6 — 8

7 — 9

8 — 7

9 — 10

10 — 9

Use what you know about pairs to 10 to make pairs that make 100p (£1).

Adding three numbers

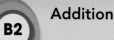

Write the total.

1. $7 + 3 + 4 = 14$

1. 7 4 3

2. 8 6 2

3. 1 9 8

4. 9 5 5

5. 2 6 4

6. 3 5 7

Write the answer.

7.
4 people get on the bus.

6 more people get on.

4 more get on. How many on the bus now?

8.
Sam has 4 marbles. He adds 3 more.

Suzie adds 5 more.

Emma adds another 6 marbles.

How many marbles now?

Make up your own story that uses addition.

Block graphs

Colours of counters

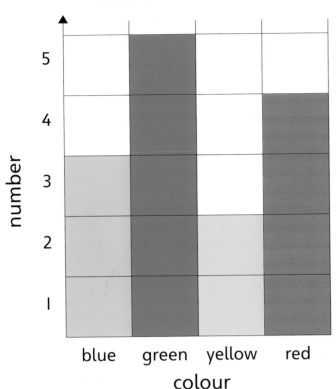

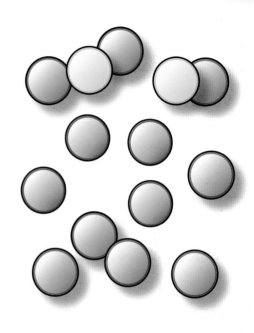

Use the graph to write the number of:

1   red counters

2   blue counters

3   yellow counters

4   green counters

5   blue and green counters

6   green and yellow counters

7   blue and red counters

8   green and red counters

9   counters altogether

10   counters that are not red

Draw your own block graph for blue, green, red and yellow counters. Make sure there are 18 counters altogether.

Pictographs

Number of ice-creams sold

strawberry	🍦	🍦	🍦	🍦		
vanilla	🍦	🍦	🍦	🍦	🍦	
mint	🍦	🍦				
chocolate	🍦	🍦	🍦	🍦	🍦	🍦

🍦 = 1 ice-cream

Write the number of ice-creams sold that are:

1 mint   2 strawberry

3 chocolate   4 vanilla

5 mint or chocolate

6 vanilla or strawberry.

7 Write the number of ice-creams sold altogether.

Ice-creams cost 15p each. How much does the ice-cream man get for the strawberry ice-creams he has sold? For the vanilla ice-creams? For all the ice-creams?

3D shapes

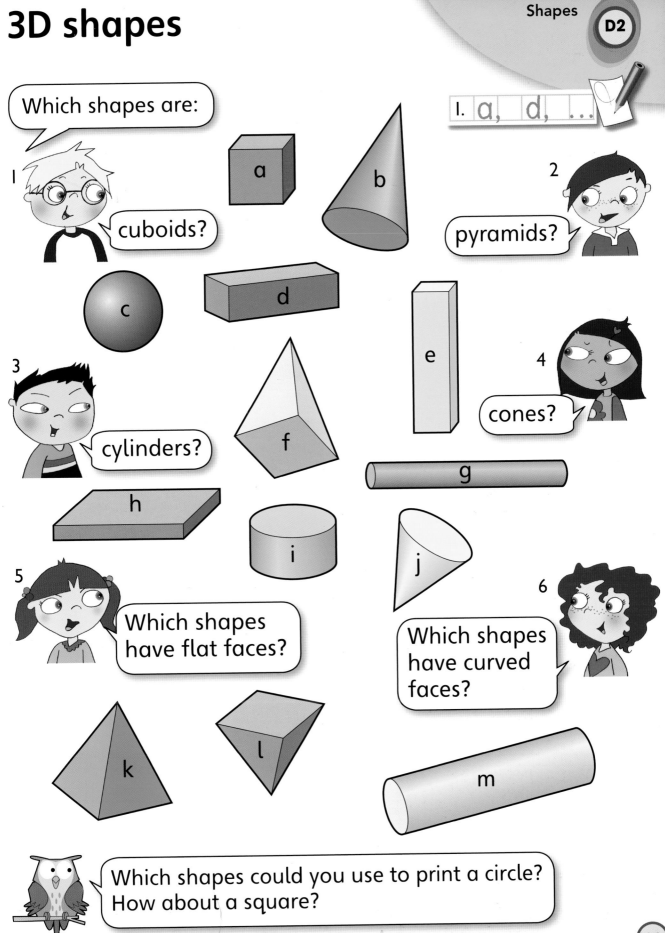

Which shapes are:

1. cuboids?

2. pyramids?

3. cylinders?

4. cones?

5. Which shapes have flat faces?

6. Which shapes have curved faces?

1. a, d, ...

Which shapes could you use to print a circle?
How about a square?

3D shapes

Counting back in 10s

Take off 30p from each price. Write the new prices.

I. 1 7 p

1 47p

2 62p

3 59p

86p

£1·71

4

5

SALE

99p

7

6

£1·53

Write the next three amounts.

8. 3 4 p, 2 4 p, 1 4 p

8 64p 54p 44p

9 £1·68 £1·58 £1·48

10 £2·70 £2·60 £2·50

11 £1·52 £1·42 £1·32

12 £3·99 £3·89 £3·79

Look at each price less than £1. How much change would you get from £1?

Adding or subtracting 9

Add 9p to each price.

1. $28p + 9p = 37p$

28p

64p

72p

56p

37p

83p

2

Take off 9p from each price.

2. $28p - 9p = 19p$

---

3 Lee is 8. Amy is 5.

How old will they be in 9 years?

---

4 9 more cars join the line.

How many cars now?

---

5 Cut 9 cm off each ribbon.

18 cm   24 cm   38 cm
Write their new lengths.

---

6 Each kitten gains 19 grams.

247 g   328 g   164 g
Write their new weights.

Odd and even

Write the next odd number after each door number.

1. `1 2 5`

1   124

2   137

3   142

4   219

5   99

6   327

Write the next even number.

7. `1 3 6`

7   135

8   117

9   264

10   378

11   98

12   132

Find how many 2-digit numbers have digits that are both odd, for example 37 or 91.
How many numbers have digits that are both even?

15

Twos and fives

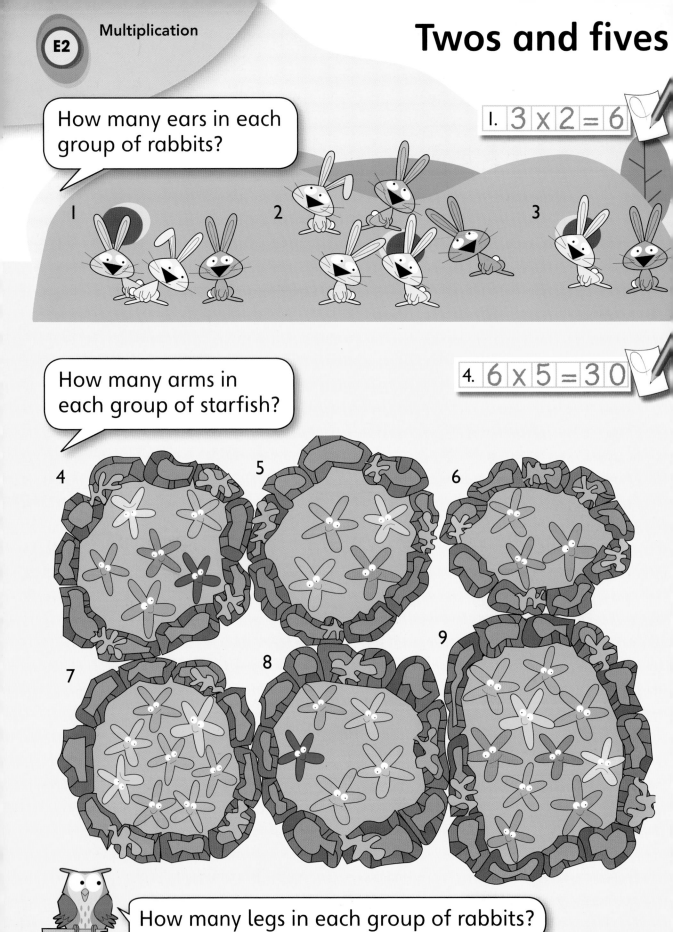

How many ears in each group of rabbits?

1. $3 \times 2 = 6$

How many arms in each group of starfish?

4. $6 \times 5 = 30$

How many legs in each group of rabbits?

Multiplying and dividing

How many beads on each frame?

I. $3 \times 4 = 12$

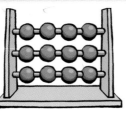

1

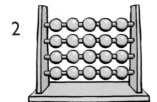

2

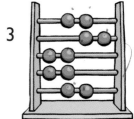

3

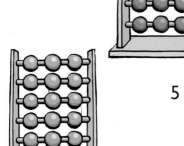

4

5

6

7 Jumbo has 4 packets of 3 buns.

How many buns in all?

8 There are 3 pots, each with 6 flowers.

How many flowers altogether?

9 There are 5 bugs on each leaf.

How many bugs in total?

10 There are 4 cakes, each with 5 candles.

How many candles are there?

Dividing

How many monsters behind each curtain?

1. $2 \times 4 = 8$

1
 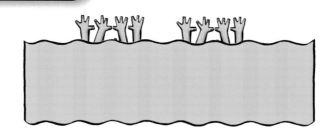 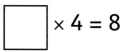

☐ × 4 = 8

2

☐ × 2 = 10

3

☐ × 4 = 12

4

☐ × 5 = 15

5
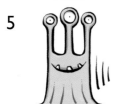 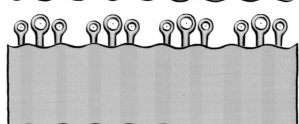

☐ × 3 = 12

I have 24 monster eggs. How many boxes of 6? What other sizes of box would hold them all?

6 monster eggs

Hundreds, tens and units

Copy and write the missing numbers.

I. $100 + 30 + 4 = 134$

1 $\boxed{1\ 0\ 0}$ + $\boxed{3\ 0}$ + $\boxed{}$ = $\boxed{1\ 3\ 4}$

$\boxed{2\ 0\ 0}$

2 $\boxed{2\ 0\ 0}$ + $\boxed{6\ 0}$ + $\boxed{4}$ = $\boxed{}$

3 $\boxed{4\ 0\ 0}$ + $\boxed{}$ + $\boxed{7}$ = $\boxed{4\ 8\ 7}$

4 $\boxed{}$ + $\boxed{7\ 0}$ + $\boxed{5}$ = $\boxed{2\ 7\ 5}$

5 $\boxed{5\ 0\ 0}$ + $\boxed{}$ = $\boxed{5\ 8\ 0}$

6 $\boxed{3\ 0}$ + $\boxed{4\ 0\ 0}$ + $\boxed{7}$ = $\boxed{}$

$\boxed{7}$

7 $\boxed{}$ + $\boxed{}$ + $\boxed{6\ 0\ 0}$ = $\boxed{6\ 4\ 2}$

8 $\boxed{}$ + $\boxed{4\ 0\ 0}$ + $\boxed{7}$ = $\boxed{4\ 2\ 7}$

9 $\boxed{}$ + $\boxed{3\ 0\ 0}$ = $\boxed{3\ 7\ 0}$

10 $\boxed{}$ + $\boxed{1}$ + $\boxed{}$ = $\boxed{5\ 6\ 1}$

$\boxed{6\ 0}$

How many 3-digit numbers less than 500 have a 0 in the 10s place?

Rounding

Round each jump to the nearest 10 centimetres.

I. 20 cm

1
18 cm

2
43 cm

3
21 cm

4
57 cm

5
65 cm

6
34 cm

7
29 cm

8
47 cm

9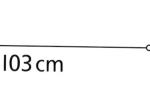
103 cm

10
118 cm

If one number rounds to 20 and another one rounds to 30, what could the exact total of the two numbers be?

Adding

Tom's dog Buster has walked over his work!
Write the number hidden by Buster's footprints.

1. $28 + 4 = 32$

1   $28 + 4 =$

2   $39 + 5 =$

3   $17 + = 23$

4   $29 + = 31$

5   $46 + = 50$

6   $58 + 3 =$

7   $27 + 5 =$

8   $37 + = 41$

9   $19 + = 23$

10   $38 + 5 =$

11   $49 + 3 =$

12   $45 + = 51$

Find different numbers that could
be hidden by these footprints:

$2 + = 3$

Difference

Write the difference between the scores.

1. **3 points**

1
John	Ruth
28	31

2
Max	Jane
17	23

3
Ali	Steve
42	38

4
Reena	Helen
24	19

5
Adam	Jo
18	23

6
Jack	Aysha
57	62

7
Liz	Raj
52	46

8
Sam	Katie
103	95

Two numbers between 20 and 40 have a difference of 6. What could they be?

Shape patterns

Use cubes to build each shape.

How many faces?

1

2

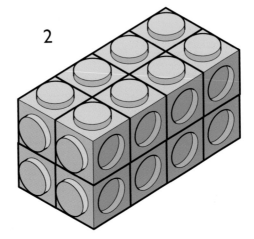

3

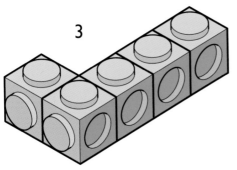

4

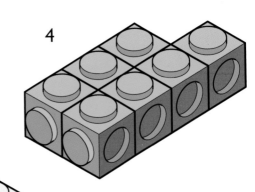

5

6

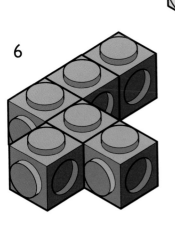

7

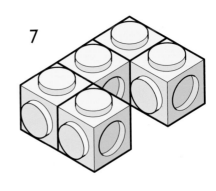

Make some shapes with 10 faces.

Fractions

Draw each shape. Divide it into halves, then into quarters.

1.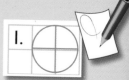

1

2

3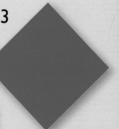

4

5

6 Ali has 16 marbles. He gives $\frac{1}{4}$ each to his 4 friends.

How many marbles each?

7 Sean has to give $\frac{1}{4}$ of his pocket money to his sister.

How much must he give her?

8 Ashley is 12 years old. He has lived half his life in the city and half his life in the country.

How many years did he live in the city?

9 Cinema tickets are £4. Jade's mum says she must pay half.

PRICE   DATE   PROGRAMME TIME
£4   3 DEC   10:45

LORD OF THE KINGS

SCREEN   ROW   SEAT
5   **E**   **3**

CINEMA

How much does Jade pay?

Making 10 and 100

Write the hidden numbers.

I. 3

1   __ + 7 = 10

2   __ + 1 = 10

3   3 + __ = 10

4   __ + 5 = 10

5   6 + __ = 10

6   2 + __ = 10

7   __ + 10 = 100

8   __ + 30 = 100

9   50 + __ = 100

10   80 + __ = 100

11   __ + 40 = 100

12   70 + __ = 100

13   __ + 90 = 100

14   0 + __ = 100

15   __ + 60 = 100

16   __ + 10 = 100

Make pairs to 100 using 'fives', for example 5, 15, 25, 35...

Making the next 10

How much more to make 20p?

1. 8 p

1  2  3

4  5   6

How much more to make 30p?

7. 7 p

7  8  9

10  11  12

How much more to make 50p?

13. 5 p

13  14  15

16  17  18

 Make the next 10p for these questions using the fewest coins possible.

Adding and subtracting

Write how many paper-clips are left in the box.

I. $400 - 3 = 397$

1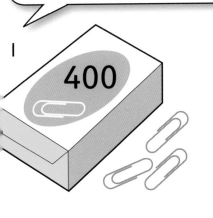
400

2
700

3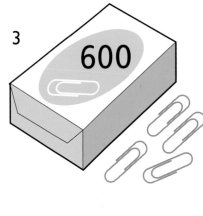
600

4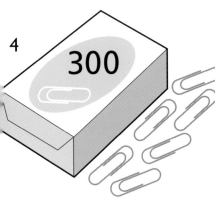
300

5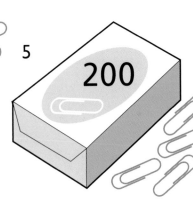
200

6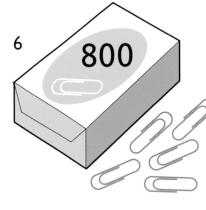
800

7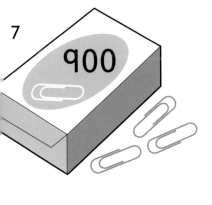
900

8
500

9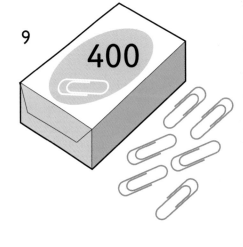
400

 Subtract 104 paper-clips from each box.

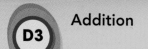
Adding

Write the total number of loaves in each batch.

1. 28 + 12 = 40

1 28 white 12 brown

2 54 white 24 brown

3 46 brown 23 white

4 27 white 15 brown

5 38 brown 14 white

6 48 brown 23 white

7 45 white 16 brown

8 57 white 36 brown

9 39 white 25 brown

10 36 white 26 brown

11 43 brown 17 white

12 29 white 13 brown

The baker baked at least 25 white loaves and at least 25 brown loaves. He baked 62 loaves altogether. How many white and brown loaves could there be?

Subtracting

Class 2 have been baking and selling cakes. Write how many each child has left to sell.

1. $35 - 21 = 14$

1 Amy
35 baked
21 sold

2 Reena
27 baked
14 sold

3 Raghu
46 baked
24 sold

4 Josh
58 baked
23 sold

5 Lizzie
47 baked
35 sold

6 Asif
29 baked
23 sold

7 James
38 baked
24 sold

8 Matt
45 baked
31 sold

9 Helen
56 baked
43 sold

If each cake costs 10p, how much has each person collected?

Dyvyding

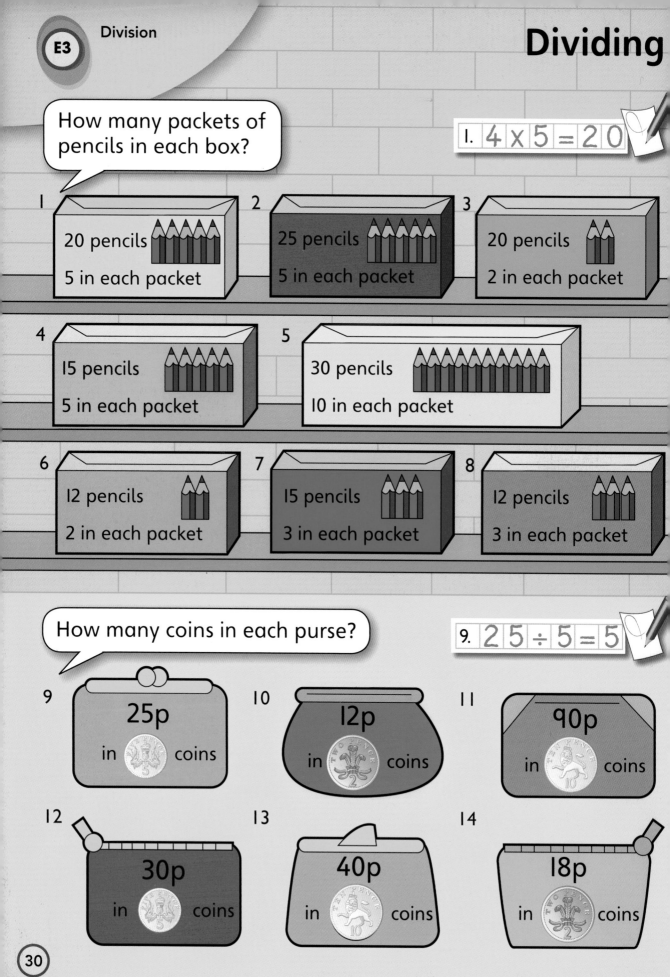

How many packets of pencils in each box?

1. 4 × 5 = 20

1. 20 pencils 5 in each packet
2. 25 pencils 5 in each packet
3. 20 pencils 2 in each packet
4. 15 pencils 5 in each packet
5. 30 pencils 10 in each packet
6. 12 pencils 2 in each packet
7. 15 pencils 3 in each packet
8. 12 pencils 3 in each packet

How many coins in each purse?

9. 25 ÷ 5 = 5

9. 25p in ___ coins
10. 12p in ___ coins
11. 90p in ___ coins
12. 30p in ___ coins
13. 40p in ___ coins
14. 18p in ___ coins

Multiplying and dividing

Write how many pieces of fruit.

1. $6 \times 5 = 30$

1

2

3

4

5

6

7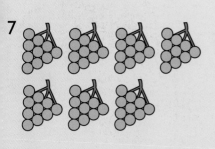

8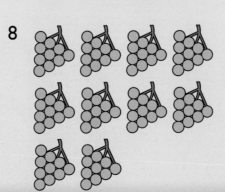

9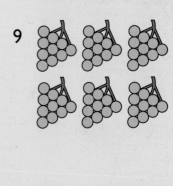

10 Greg has 3 packets of football stickers.

Zoë gives him 4 pairs of stickers.

Sunil gives him 5 more.

How many stickers does Greg have now?

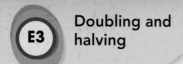

Doubling and halving

Double each child's score.

1 15

2 20

3 45

4 30

5 35

6 50

Find half of the money in each purse.

7

8

9

10

Start with 64p. How many times can you split this amount in half?